FAMILY BUDGETS T H A T WORK

LARRY BURKETT

Tyndale House Publishers, Inc.
Wheaton, Illinois

Adapted from *What Husbands Wish Their Wives Knew about Money,* copyright 1977 by SP Publications, Inc. Used by permission. Additional material is taken from *The Financial Planning Workbook,* copyright 1979 by Christian Financial Concepts. Used by permission.

Scripture quotations are from the *New American Standard Bible,* copyright 1960, 1962, 1963, 1968, 1971, 1972, 1973, 1975, 1977 by The Lockman Foundation.

Pocket Guide is a trademark of Tyndale House Publishers, Inc.
Library of Congress Catalog Card Number 88-50086
ISBN 0-8423-0829-6
Printed in the United States of America
95 94 93 92
11 10 9 8

CONTENTS

Financial Problems: How They Start

"Can you help us?" pleaded Ann, a petite, twenty-five-year-old mother of two who had been referred to me by her pastor. As she described her situation, she frequently remarked that she just could not understand how she and her husband had gotten into such a mess. She continually asked if I could help her.

Ann's desperate statements reflect two common occurrences today: Many families get into dire financial problems without realizing when and how they started; and, most people in that situation seek instant solutions.

A CASE STUDY
Larry and Jane were an "average" couple: young, talented, and unhappy. After enjoying happy years early in their marriage, they found financial "success" had caused their relationship to disintegrate into bitter loneliness. Their story seems to be an example of many families today.

Jane had helped to put Larry through college by working during his last two years. Early in their marriage, they had the kind of relationship that most young couples dream about. It was built upon trust, love, and communication.

Shortly after graduation, Larry was drafted into the service. During that time they had little or no money. In spite of that, those years were the happiest of their lives. In the evenings, they would talk for hours about the events of the day and of the plans they had for their future children, Larry's job, a home, and their lives together. Their dream was that one day Larry would own a business in which he and Jane could work together.

With no extra money, they spent their free time at the town zoo. Before Larry's tour was completed, they were on a first-name basis with most of the animals. After feeding the animals, they often would invest half of their total net worth on a hamburger shared together.

FINANCIAL SUCCESS

After release from the service, Larry was hired by an engineering firm as a trainee. For the next two years, he settled into the task of "getting ahead." As he got raises and promotions, Larry and Jane found they were able to buy a few previously unaffordable luxuries.

The first change in direction came after Larry was promoted to full engineer. As they began to entertain and be entertained by others in the company, Jane became aware that their furnishings didn't measure up to those of their friends. More and more she felt they had to "look successful" if they were to "be successful." As they still had very little surplus money, credit seemed to be a reasonable alternative. After all, it would be an "investment" in their future, wouldn't it?

With Jane convinced, Larry surrendered. It would be a good investment to get some of the things they needed for the future. The first investment, Larry said, had to be a car. Jane agreed, on the understanding that she could also buy some things for the house. Unfortunately, they didn't like the kind of car they could afford, so they settled on a used luxury model. Jane remodeled the living room with money borrowed from a finance company, and by the time the spending spree ceased, nearly every available dollar was committed.

TROUBLE STARTS

Then the long decline started. First, the car broke down and took extra money one month; then the insurance came due and was slightly higher so they dipped into their savings; then Jane got ill and had to be hospitalized. Almost without realizing it, they were under financial pressure. For the first time in their lives, Jane and Larry had an argument.

When Larry got the doctor's bill, he really blew his stack. "A $400 doctor bill, that's stupid! No doctor in the world is worth that! This has got to stop!" he shouted.

Jane retorted, "It's not my doctor bill that's the problem; it's your stupid car!"

That evening, there was another first in their lives. Larry and Jane stopped being companions and became adversaries. By the next morning, the whole thing seemed to have blown over, but that wasn't the end of it. You can be sure that this trend, once started, will progress on its own.

About three months later, the supervisor of Larry's department left to go to another company. Larry was approached about taking over his position. Larry and Jane were both ecstatic about the promotion; now he was really moving up in the company.

With the new position came $100 a month raise. "Just what we needed to get out of debt," Larry chortled. The words were hardly out of his mouth when their car broke down again. This time the bill would be over a hundred dollars, according to the mechanic. "We can't afford to keep this car," Larry told Jane. "It costs too much to operate it, so let's trade for a smaller one."

"We are not buying a new car while I have to suffer with these antique appliances," Jane shouted. "I'd like to have a little help around here, too. Larry, you're just being selfish." Larry then blew up at her and they yelled at each other for the second time in their lives.

The next morning they didn't communicate much. When Larry went off to work, Jane cried most of the day. That evening, Jane told him she was sorry. Larry said he was sorry, too, and that maybe there was a way they could do what both wanted. What was the solution? Buy a washer and dryer on credit payments for twenty-four months, and buy a car as well.

With the best of intentions, they began to look for a small, inexpensive car that fit their budget. Unfortunately for them, the small cars were placed on the lots next to full-size luxury models. After a short comparison, Larry decided the best buy would be a new car that would last longer and would save on repair bills. They traded their old car in and financed a new car for nearly three years at $300 a month. But they were both happy (at least temporarily) and seemed to have solved their differences.

FINANCIAL PRESSURES

About three months later, the financial pressures began to build again. Larry began to question Jane about everything she spent. They argued about groceries, light bills, dental bills, and especially cars, washers, and dryers. They began to pick each other apart. The worse their married life became, the worse their finances became, and vice versa.

They found themselves forced to borrow more money just to survive on a month-to-month basis. As one credit card came due, another would be used to pay it. Then they began to buy perishables such as food and clothing on credit and drifted deeper and deeper into debt. The more intense the pressure from debts became, the more they would argue and blame each other.

Jane began to feel relief when Larry left in the morning. This frightened her, as she realized that she was not happy about Larry anymore and actually looked forward to being away from him. Larry began to come home later and later in the evenings and would seldom communicate at all. They began to drift apart and assume an attitude of distrust.

Their marriage was becoming a battlefield. Jane would go to bed at night with a knot in the pit of her stomach and Larry went to bed with anger written all over his face. When he got paid on Fridays and tried to balance their checkbook, his anger really flared. They had checks returned for insufficient funds because Jane failed to keep good records. Creditors began calling her at home.

Fortunately for Larry and Jane, their marriage meant enough to them that they sought help. I shared with Larry and Jane over the next few months the same plan shared later in this book. It is not my plan but God's: taken from his Word, it is both simple and practical. The result of this plan in the lives of Larry and Jane was to bring them back together. Not only did they find a solution to their financial problems but also the solution to their marriage problems.

COMMON COPING PATTERNS

Most American marriages begin with the great expectations of two people who wish to share their lives together. Nearly half of these marriages fail, with miserable, bitter people the result. Why do relationships that begin with so much hope go wrong?

In more than 70 percent of the marriages that fail, the primary "symptom" is finances. Under the best circumstances, conflicts between a man and a woman who share the same home are inevitable. When a relationship is strained by constant financial pressures, the result is usually open hostility and bitterness. These emotions may be just the beginning of pressures on the home.

Divorce. Many couples faced with the decision about whether to solve the problems or run find it easier to run. They rationalize that it must be the other person's fault and that somehow the problems would miraculously disappear if they were separated. But this "solution" usually doesn't work. I have counseled many couples in their second marriages who were back in the midst of crises very similar to the ones they had left.

Mental illness. When living in continuing stress, many people become so fearful and depressed they exhibit signs of mental illness. Not everyone, of course, needs hospitalization; most simply withdraw from responsibility and refuse to be a part of any decisions.

The Ostrich Method. When a family has previously attempted to treat their financial symptoms and failed to solve the problems, a great temptation is to ignore the fact that the symptoms have reappeared. People who attempt this end up in even greater trouble because creditors will not buy the ostrich method.

I recognized the symptom when I answered

an urgent phone call one evening. The young man on the other end of the line said he urgently needed help. He had just been served a "garnishment of wages" summons and was required to appear in court within five days for the judge to set the amount. His plea was, "What can I do now? I'm afraid my boss will fire me."

I asked him how old the debt in question was and when he had last paid on it. It turned out the debt was over a year old and no payment or contact had been made for nearly eight months. His reason was, he said, "I didn't have enough money to make the whole payment every month and I didn't think they would accept a lesser amount." I then asked if he had received a copy of the original court summons when the creditor had filed suit. His reply was the same; yes, he had, but since he didn't have the money to pay the debt he simply didn't show up in court.

The old ostrich method was working beautifully. Unfortunately, ignoring a problem will not make it go away. It always returns worse than before.

Bankruptcy. Bankruptcy is a legal means of avoiding creditors by declaring oneself to be insolvent financially.

The legal rules of bankruptcy are established by state law and thus vary from state to state, but the intent is fairly consistent. Once the court has determined that an individual owes more than he can repay, all assets are liquidated and distributed to the creditors. From that point on, no creditor may collect further payment.

This escape is also temporary. Since an individual filing bankruptcy cannot do so again for six years, he is immediately supplied with readily available credit. Many times the very companies that have just lost what was owed during the bankruptcy are the first new creditors.

Religious escape. A religious escape occurs when someone having great financial problems joins a group of people who are oblivious to any practical concern for material possessions. The result is that the financial problems are thought to be punishment for religious convictions, and therefore not worthy of further consideration.

Linda was a mother of two, slightly over thirty years old, and seemingly very religious. Her husband, Jack, was distraught over the fact that Linda would not accept any responsibility for finances in the home, even to the point of balancing her checkbook. Her answer for everything was, "Don't worry about it. God will provide."

God does provide; everything we have comes from him. But he also directs us to use our abilities and to be responsible for our actions. When one turns to God for help, more responsibility is expected, not less. The Bible says, "And if you have not been faithful in the use of that which is another's, who will give you that which is your own?" (Luke 16:12). Linda's actions reflected an escape mechanism rather than a commitment to God.

THE ROOT PROBLEM: ATTITUDE

The root problem of financial problems, with various alterations, is *attitude*. The attitude may be greed, covetousness, ignorance, indulgence, or impatience. Some people are ingenious enough to combine two or more of these attitudes, but the result is always the same: financial bondage.

WANTING THE BEST

Greed can be defined as always wanting more and pride as wanting the "best."

Have you noticed how few people seem to be truly satisfied with what they have? That is why there is such a demand for bigger and shinier gadgets. Most families adjust their spending based on the availability of money, either borrowed or earned, not on needs.

Available money enables a family to expand its stock of goods far beyond what reason dictates. To verify this, one has only to shop at a few neighborhood garage sales. You will find very expensive items available for almost nothing. Why? Their owners bought them on impulse and found they had no use for them.

Famous name brands are developed to take advantage of the attitude of pride. It is interesting that men and women are willing to pay more at an exclusive shop for the same articles they could buy for much less at a good department store.

How are the attitudes of greed and pride conquered? By establishing good plans so that you can recognize when you have enough.

Jesus said, "Beware, and be on your guard against every form of greed; for not even when one has an abundance does his life consist of his possessions" (Luke 12:15).

KEEPING UP WITH THE JONESES

Covetousness, an attitude of desiring what others have, is what we commonly call "keeping up with the Joneses." How many times have you caught yourself comparing your success, or the lack of it, with an old school acquaintance? Or have you actually decided to change jobs or buy a larger home because your older brother was getting ahead of you?

Covetousness is promoted in most sales programs. Many sales campaigns are based on the "bait 'em and hook 'em" scheme which relies almost exclusively on greed (wanting the best) and covetousness (someone else wants it too). When a couple reads about that "great little car" in the newspaper, they hurry down to the dealer expecting to find what was advertised. "Oh, you wanted a car with engine and wheels," says the salesman. "Well, just look at this little beauty over here." So he shuffles them over to the new car section. Knowing that they came expecting to buy a car, he also knows when they spot the one they really want.

"That's *you*," he says. "You'll be the envy of your friends in this little jewel." If they hesitate or don't seem to bite right away, he will soften them up with discounts and rebates. But his clincher is, "If you really want this car, you'd better decide now. I have a guy coming in with a deposit to hold it this afternoon."

Toward what is his closing directed? Covetousness. The simple principle to employ here is: Do not compare your family with others. If you do, you'll *always* end up in competition with someone else.

"WE DIDN'T KNOW"

Ignorant does not mean stupid; it means uninformed. For instance, many couples buy on credit without concern for the cost of the item. Their primary concern at the time is, "How much are the monthly payments?"

Others borrow more money than they can repay because they have no system of budgeting. They literally don't know where their money goes each month or how much credit their income can support.

I once assumed that almost everyone knew how to balance a checking account. I quickly discovered this was an erroneous assumption. Many people have only a vague idea of how much is in their bank accounts and have *never* balanced their accounts. They write checks and fail to record them in their ledger, they pay overdraft charges on checks written on insufficient funds, or they simply accept the bank's statement as totally accurate.

One couple was even paying for the bank's errors.

Cathy kept the "books" for their home records. After our first session, I had a strong suspicion that the books weren't being kept too well, as they regularly paid overdraft charges for insufficient funds. So I asked Cathy to bring her bank statement and ledger book the next visit.

A month had passed before we talked again and during that time two more checks had "bounced." I asked Cathy how she balanced her checkbook after she received the monthly bank statement.

"Oh, I look to be sure that every check they return is really ours." Good, no problem there.

"Next, I cross off all the returned checks in my checkbook." No problem there either, except that she forgot to mention she couldn't find all of them in her checkbook.

"Then I subtract the service charge and overdraft charges from my checkbook, deducting my outstanding checks from the bank's account, and compare my checkbook to their statement."

"Great," I said. "How do they compare?"

"Oh, they never do," replied Cathy. "So I always use the bank's figure."

Two things I discovered about this method of home accounting: (1) it is a very common method of keeping records; (2) it is grossly inaccurate.

Cathy had some enormous problems in her records. Because she didn't write down every check, she obviously couldn't subtract them from the bank's balance. Thus, there always seemed to be more money than there really was. We also discovered that the bank had actually paid the returned checks the first time through, added an insufficient funds penalty, and returned the check to the payee, who then resubmitted the check. By that time there were additional funds in the account and the check cleared, but Cathy's account was again debited the amount of the check.

So she had actually paid the checks twice, plus penalties. When we researched the bank account, we were able to recover over $200 in overpayments during the previous year. Through this lesson, Cathy became a knowledgeable record keeper.

INDULGING

The general definition of an indulgence is "a thing that has little or no utility." It is often bought on impulse and usually stands idle after purchase.

In searching for a good example, I almost always go back to the time I purchased a boat. I could have rented the *Queen Mary* on an hour-by-hour basis for the same use I got out of that boat. I suspect a great many men can identify with the same indulgence.

There are always good rationalizations for indulgences. How many people who purchased a bicycle slenderizing machine had first tried jogging? What usually happens to the $100 piece of equipment after it's paid for? It's stuck in the garage or basement and later sold for $5 at a garage sale. What about the great travel trailer for $8,000 that was going to save all that money on vacations? Usually it's used one summer and then left to depreciate on its own. I have talked to a great many couples in financial trouble who would willingly give up their

A Relationship with Christ

Have you ever committed your life to Jesus Christ? This is the vital step in solving family problems, financial or otherwise. The Bible says, "He came that you might have life and have it more abundantly" (John 10:10, paraphrased). All he asks is that you believe in him as your Savior and Lord. (See Rom. 10:9.) The principles of handling money God's way, as discussed in this book, will work for anyone. But unless the basic need for a relationship with God is met first, the root problems that led to financial bondage will appear in a different area later.

equity in boats, trailers, or motor homes, for anyone who would take over the payments.

One doctor's indulgences were steam locomotives—real ones. It had all started as a hobby a few years earlier when he was collecting antique model trains. But as his involvement increased, he ran across an individual who owned an 1860 locomotive. This fellow told him what a great investment old trains were and talked him into buying his before the big steam locomotive rush got started.

So the doctor bought not one but six locomotives. He quickly discovered that owning steam locomotives is a little like catching alligators. Once you have them it's hard to let go. By the time he owned enough of them to satisfy his desire for old trains, they were draining his finances to the tune of $1,000 a month storage. After several months of fruitless attempts to sell the engines, he decided to give some away. After several months of no success at giving them away (because of the moving costs), he finally had to pay several organizations to take them.

There is a deceptively simple principle to observe concerning indulgences: Do not buy things that have little or no utility to you. Before you buy something, identify your *need* for the item, allocate money for it, thoroughly search out the best buy, and pray about whether or not you should make the purchase. (See page 52.)

GETTING RICH QUICK

A wise proverb says, "A man with an evil eye hastens after wealth, and does not know that want will come upon him." Many families have been wiped out financially because of a "get-rich-quick" attitude. The schemes for accommodating this attitude are as varied as human ingenuity. The common thread running through them? Make a lot of money—quickly— with very little effort.

Thus, the doctor is attracted to buy into an oil well, a chicken farm, or a movie. The athlete is sold a car wash franchise or the preacher a distributorship for motivational programs. The interesting common characteristic is that the get-rich-quick scheme is almost always outside the investor's normal skill area. Then why does he get into it? Because he thinks the grass is greener on the other side.

It is also true that many people who buy into most get-rich-quick schemes risk borrowed money. Most promoters challenge prospects to borrow by attacking their reluctance as timidity. "If you don't take a chance, you'll never get ahead." It has a good ring to it, doesn't it?

One of the most far-reaching get-rich-quick programs ever created is the stock market. I don't mean to imply that everyone in the stock market is trying to get rich quick. Some people are experts and invest according to sound business and scriptural principles. But many others are involved in an area they know virtually nothing about, risking money they cannot afford to lose (often borrowed), and making decisions based on whims.

Before I am besieged by irate stockbrokers, let me say I am not debasing the stock market itself. For many wise and knowledgeable business investors, it is a useful instrument. I know many people who have made money consistently in the market. They were expert investors. But I have known many more people who lost money they could not afford to risk.

This same principle may apply to land syndications, fast-food franchises, gold bullion, freeze-dried foods, or anything else where the product sales are de-emphasized and the get-rich-quick aspect is promoted.

How can one avoid these traps?

1. Never risk money you cannot afford to lose.

2. Never get involved with things you don't understand.
3. Demand sufficient information to evaluate thoroughly the business.
4. Seek good, noninvolved Christian counsel.
5. Set a minimum time to pray and seek God's direction.

The Basics of Family Budgets

Who needs a budget? Obviously, those who are in debt. They're spending more than they make. A budget is a plan to balance spending with income.

But those who are not in debt need a budget, too, because a budget is also a plan for controlling spending. A budget should help determine how much can be cut back to develop a surplus. There is virtually no way to avoid financial problems without some kind of planning. A budget is a plan to manage your money.

People have two common tendencies when beginning to plan. The first is to establish plans and then never follow them. The second is to establish unrealistic plans that allow nothing for a balanced family life. Both of these lead to more frustration and eventual discouragement. Your plans must be both realistic and applied to be fruitful.

It's interesting that none of the couples who have come to me for financial counseling were on a budget. Some had made out a budget and promptly filed it away in their bureau drawer.

Others had made out an unrealistic budget that provided nothing for clothing, entertainment, dental or medical care, and so forth. It also became unusable in a very short time.

A budget is made to be used and must therefore be realistic. It should be a plan for managing *your* finances, not someone else's.

DETERMINING MONTHLY INCOME AND EXPENSES

Planning a budget means more than just writing figures down on a piece of paper. It means sitting down and talking about the current situation, where you need to go, and how you are going to get there. If you have children old enough to understand, they can be included in your budget discussion.

The present condition. A budget discussion must begin with the current situation. Perhaps you have never sat down and figured out how much money you make and how much you spend every month. On the Monthly Income and Expenses form (figure 2.1), you can compare actual monthly expenses with monthly income to determine your present spending.

Income per month. List all gross income (income before tax deductions) in the "Income per Month" section on the Monthly Income and Expenses form. Don't forget to consider commissions, bonuses, fees, tips, periodic savings withdrawals, allowances, gifts, and loans.

If you operate on a nonfixed monthly income, such as sales or commissions, divide the previ-

Keeping an Expense Diary

Some families may not know how much they are presently spending. In that case, I recommend that both husband and wife keep an expense diary for at least thirty or sixty days. Both should carry a small diary everywhere they go and write down all expenditures, even down to a dime.

At the end of every month, list each expenditure under the appropriate category. Then, at the end of a month or two, evaluate how much you are *actually* spending in each area. The effort of writing expenses down will probably help to control your spending somewhat, but additionally, it will provide a very accurate picture of your current spending.

ous year's salary by twelve to get a month-by-month budget income. Don't forget to deduct taxes and other prepayments that are due. If you are paid on a weekly or bi-weekly basis, take the total yearly income and divide it by twelve.

Business expense reimbursements should not be considered family income. Avoid the trap of using expense money to buffer family spending or the result will be an indebtedness that cannot be paid.

Net spendable income. Net spendable income is that portion of your income available for family spending. Some of your income does not belong to the family and therefore cannot be spent. For instance:

- The tithe: This assures that the first tenth of your income goes to God. (For a detailed discussion of tithing, see chapter 10 of *Your Finances in Changing Times* by Larry Burkett, Moody Press.)

- Taxes: Federal withholding, social security, and state and local taxes must also be deducted from gross income. Self-employed individuals must not forget to set aside money for quarterly payments on taxes. Beware of the tendency to treat unpaid tax money as windfall profit.

- Other deductions: Payroll deductions for insurance, credit union savings, or debt payments, as well as bonds, stock programs, retirement, and union dues can be handled in either of two ways:
  1. Treat them as a deduction from your gross income.
  2. Include them in spendable income and deduct them from the proper category. This way is preferred because it provides a more accurate picture of where the money is being spent.

Example: A deduction is being made for credit union savings. This amount should be considered as a part of income with an expense shown under "Savings" for the same amount. This method makes it easier to see the overall effect the deduction has on the family budget.

Monthly expenses. List your expenditures in the home on a monthly basis.

- Housing expenses: All monthly expenses necessary to operate the home, including taxes, insurance, maintenance, and utilities. The amount used for utility payments should be an average monthly amount for the past twelve months. If you cannot establish an accurate maintenance expense, use 10 percent of the monthly mortgage payment.
- Food expenses: All grocery expenses, including paper goods and nonfood products normally purchased at grocery stores. Include milk, bread, and items purchased in addition to regular shopping trips. *Do not* include meals eaten out.
- Automobile expenses: Includes payments, insurance, gas, oil, maintenance, and depreciation. Depreciation is actually the money set aside to repair or replace the automobile. The minimum amount set aside should be sufficient to keep the car in decent repair and to replace it at least every four to five years. If replacement funds are not available in the budget, the minimum allocation should be maintenance costs. Annual or semi-annual auto insurance payments should be set aside on a monthly basis, thereby avoiding the crisis of a neglected expense.
- Insurance: Includes all insurance—such as health, life, and disability—not associated with the home or auto.
- Debts: Includes all monthly payments required to meet debt obligations. Home mort-

MONTHLY INCOME AND EXPENSES

Income per Month
    Salary   _____
    Interest   _____
    Dividends   _____
    Notes   _____
    Rents   _____
Total Gross Income   _____

Less:
  1. Tithe   _____
  2. Tax   _____

Net Spendable Income   _____
  3. Housing   _____
    Mortgage (rent)   _____
    Insurance   _____
    Taxes   _____
    Electricity   _____
    Gas   _____
    Water   _____
    Sanitation   _____
    Telephone   _____
    Maintenance   _____
    Other   _____
  4. Food   _____
  5. Automobile(s)   _____
    Payments   _____
    Gas & Oil   _____
    Insurance   _____
    License   _____
    Taxes   _____
    Maint./Repair/
      Replacement   _____
  6. Insurance   _____
    Life   _____
    Medical   _____
    Other   _____

7. **Debts** _____
    Credit Card _____
    Loans & Notes _____
    Other _____
 8. **Enter. & Recreation** _____
    Eating Out _____
    Trips _____
    Baby-sitters _____
    Activities _____
    Vacation _____
    Other _____
 9. **Clothing** _____
10. **Savings** _____
11. **Medical Expenses** _____
    Doctor _____
    Dentist _____
    Drugs _____
    Other _____
12. **Miscellaneous** _____
    Toiletry, cosmetics _____
    Beauty, barber _____
    Laundry, cleaning _____
    Allowances, lunches _____
    Subscriptions _____
    Gifts (incl.
      Christmas) _____
    Special Education _____
    Cash _____
    Other _____

Total Expenses ========

Income vs. Expense
      Net Spendable Income _____
      Less Expenses _____
      ========

Figure 2.1

gage and automobile payments are not included here.

- Entertainment and recreation: Vacation savings, camping trips, club dues, sporting equipment, hobby expenses, and athletic events. Don't forget expenses associated with Little League, booster clubs, and so on.
- Clothing: The average annual amount spent on clothes divided by twelve. The minimum amount should be at least ten dollars per month per family member.
- Savings: Every family should allocate something for savings. A savings account can provide funds for emergencies and is a key element in good planning and financial freedom.
- Medical expenses: Insurance deductibles, doctors' bills, eyeglasses, drugs, orthodontist visits, and so forth. Use a yearly average divided by twelve to determine a monthly amount.
- Miscellaneous: Unusual expenses that do not seem to fit anywhere else—day-care expenses for working mothers, special or private education costs, pocket allowance (coffee money), gifts, Christmas presents, and so forth. Miscellaneous spending is usually underestimated. (See page 56.)

Where do you stand? Add the expenses under each of the major categories (items 3 through 12) and note this figure as total expenses. In the space provided, subtract expenses from net spendable income. If your income is greater than your expenses, you then have only to implement a plan that will help you meet your financial goals. If your expenses are greater than your income, you will need to evaluate every category to decide whether or not you are overspending and, if so, how spending can be reduced. The following section will help you do this.

CHECKING YOUR SPENDING

In this section we will break key expenses into recommended percentages of income. The guidelines here can serve as a basis for determining areas of overspending in your budget that are creating the greatest problems. Additionally, they can be used as a goal for budgeting. Be aware that these percentages are not absolutes, they are only guidelines. But they do help to establish the upper levels of spending.

The percentages given are based on an income of between $18,000 and $28,000 a year for a family of four. (See pages 32-33 for a percentage guide based on other family incomes.) The budget has been adjusted by deducting 10 percent of the gross for tithe and 20 percent for taxes, leaving net spendable income. The percentages given will equal 100 percent of net spendable income.

HOUSING

For the salary range described above, housing should constitute approximately 30 percent of the spendable income.

PERCENTAGE GUIDE FOR FAMILY INCOME

	28,000	32,000	40,000	50,000	60,000
Gross Income					
Tithe	10%	10%	10%	10%	10%
Taxes	20%	22%	24%	26%	30%
NET SPENDABLE	19,600	21,760	26,400	32,000	36,000
Housing	30%	30%	28%	25%	25%
Auto	15%	15%	12%	12%	12%
Food	16%	16%	14%	14%	10%
Insurance	5%	5%	5%	5%	5%

Entertainment/Rec.	7%	7%	7%	7%	7%	7%
Clothing	5%	5%	5%	5%	6%	6%
Medical/Dental	5%	5%	4%	4%	4%	4%
Miscellaneous	6%	7%	7%	7%	8%	8%
Savings	5%	5%	5%	5%	5%	5%
Debts	6%	5%	5%	5%	5%	5%
Investments	—	—	8%	8%	9%	13%

Figure 2.2

In some areas of the country, housing will cost more than the allocated 30 percent. It is possible to spend as much as 40 percent of your net spendable income and still balance your budget if the additional amount can be gleaned from some of the other categories. Once the expenditure for a home exceeds 40 percent, however, it is virtually impossible to balance the budget within the salary range presented. In this circumstance, there is probably no alternative but to move to less expensive living quarters.

Unfortunately, housing is the largest budget problem of most families, particularly young families. The median income in the United States in 1987 was $18,900. The average house in America in 1987 cost approximately $100,000. A family making $18,900 a year would have to spend approximately 50 percent of their income to buy a $100,000 home—virtually impossible.

It's distressing that many couples have been talked into buying a home long before they could afford it. They have neither the down payment nor the monthly payments. (See page 81 for cost-saving tips when shopping for a home.)

FOOD

Naturally an important part of a budget, food should constitute approximately 16 percent of the net spendable income of our example family. Food is probably the most flexible part of any budget, so when overspending occurs in other areas such as housing, automobiles, or insurance, the food budget is usually cut.

The reduction of food bills requires both thought and planning. Perhaps the best method you can follow is to make daily menus and buy food according to the needs of the menus. The average family eats about twenty-two different kinds of meals. Thus, you need only purchase the ingredients for about twenty-two basic menus. The amount of food you buy is then limited to nutritional requirements, not indulgence. (See page 80 for more cost-saving tips.)

AUTOMOBILES

Budget allocation for automobiles is approximately 15 percent of net spendable income. For those who are making between $18,000 and $28,000 a year, 15 percent is obviously not a lot of money. It means they must be disciplined about automobiles.

We are often foolish when it comes to our machines, particularly cars. Many couples buy new cars they cannot afford and trade them in long before their utility is depleted. Those who buy new cars usually keep them less than four years. In doing so they pay the highest cost possible for an automobile. Leasing automobiles is rapidly catching on with many households that can't afford the down payment necessary on a new car. This is perhaps the most expensive means of obtaining an automobile and I highly discourage it.

Providence and a House Hunt

When my wife and I moved to Atlanta, we sold our home in Florida where we had lived for several years. As we began to look for a house in Atlanta, I thought, "Houses just cannot cost this much." But the longer we looked, the more I realized houses really did cost that much. So we moved into an apartment.

After six months in the apartment with four growing children, we decided that we weren't cut out for that much closeness and we began to search for another home. Our search took us back to the very first house we had looked at.

The house was three years old but had never been lived in. So I contacted the builder to discuss his terms. He told me, "You know, I'm tired of this house. I'll sell it for exactly what it cost me to build it three years ago."

When he told me the cost, I said, "I'm really sorry, but I can't afford that. It's out of my budget." (I explained to him that I was a Christian and believed that God would provide a house we could afford.) As we talked further, I found that he, too, was a Christian. Before we left, he said, "Tell you what I'll do. I've been making the construction loan on this house for nearly three years myself. I'll let you rent it with an option to buy for exactly what my construction loan is."

So we moved into a home for a few dollars a month more than we were paying for an apartment. However, our apartment was about 900 square feet and the house was a little over 4,000 square feet.

We had been in the home about four months when the builder suffered a fatal heart attack. About a year later, the executor of his estate called to tell me that they needed to sell the house or they would have to pay estate taxes on it. I explained that I could not buy the house for what it cost to build four years earlier.

A few weeks later the executor called again to tell me the house had been appraised for estate taxes and they would have to pay nearly the value of the house in estate taxes. I sympathized with him, but again told him that I simply could not afford the house. "It's above my budget," I said. The reply was, "Make us an offer."

I called the mortgage company where I was making the construction loan and asked them how much mortgage I could buy for what I was already paying. It turned out to be $38,000, which was promptly accepted as the purchase price of the home.

No human being could take credit for anything that happened. God understood the need in the life of the builder and matched a need in my life.

DEBTS

Debts in the average family income should constitute no more than 6 percent of the net spendable income. Obviously, it would be great if most budgets had only 6 percent of debts or less. Unfortunately, the norm in American families far exceeds this amount.

When the amount of debt exceeds 6 percent, it is difficult to balance the budget. Remember that all the percentages must add up to no more than 100 percent. When two or three of these categories are over the recommended percentage, the budget will never balance. It means that some kind of an adjustment *must* be made.

One of the most important adjustments is determining the types of items you have on credit. Consumables such as food, clothing, and gasoline are exceedingly difficult to repay. When they're gone, so is the desire to pay for them. Also, since more consumables are needed, the debts continue to pile up. Avoid accumulating any more debt of this kind.

INSURANCE

Insurance should constitute approximately 5 percent of net spendable income. This excludes house or automobile insurance but includes life insurance, health insurance, and disability. It is assumed here that those who have health insurance are part of a group plan.

It's unfortunate that so many American families have been misled in the area of insurance. Few couples really understand insurance, either how much is needed or what kind is best. The subject will be covered more fully in chapter 4.

ENTERTAINMENT AND RECREATION
This portion of family expenses should constitute approximately 7 percent of net spendable income. We're a recreation-oriented country, and that's not necessarily bad—if it's kept in proper balance. But those in debt should not use their creditors' money to entertain themselves. In doing so they violate the principle of paying what is due.

On the other hand, do not attempt to cut entertainment and recreation back to nothing in your budget simply to bring spending within reason. You shouldn't stop every outside activity, but you should seek less expensive alternatives. You may need to get rid of your boat and instead sit on a dock to fish.

I recommend that an actual envelope system be used for monthly entertainment and recreation expenditures. When you go out to eat, take the envelope with you. After you pay for the meal, put the change back into your envelope. The key is, limit your spending to what you have in the envelope.

CLOTHING
Clothing in the family budget should constitute approximately 5 percent of net spendable income. Families in debt tend to sacrifice too much in this area and buy clothes *only* in panic

Before You Shop for Clothes

As you consider your family's clothing budget, ask yourself these questions:

- Does it really matter whether you have all of the latest styles?
- Do your purchases reflect good utility rather than ego?
- Do you buy clothes to satisfy family needs or to satisfy whims and indulgences?

situations. Your family can be clothed neatly without great expense, but this requires some effort and diligence in selecting the proper clothing your family needs. It also requires maintenance of existing clothes when necessary. Teach your children to use their clothes properly and to care for them carefully.

As part of your budget planning, you should decide how much you can spend for clothing on a yearly basis, divide it by 12, and allocate that amount of money on a monthly basis. Since you will not spend the total amount of money every month, you should transfer the surplus to a savings account to be available when necessary. Thus, when clothing sales are available, you will have money from which to draw.

MEDICAL AND DENTAL EXPENSES

Approximately 5 percent of our example's income is allocated to medical and dental expenses. A family has a great advantage if it has group health insurance, but many couples do not have this benefit. Those who do not must allocate a greater amount in their budget to health-related costs. In most cases it will far exceed 5 percent.

If you fall into this category, you will need to reduce spending in another area of your budget to compensate. Medical expenses must be anticipated and the funds set aside regularly. Failure to do so will spoil budget plans and lead to indebtedness.

MISCELLANEOUS

Miscellaneous expenses should be approximately 6 percent of net spendable income. (See page 56.)

SAVINGS

It is important that you budget some savings. Otherwise, the use of credit becomes a lifelong necessity, and debt a way of life. Your savings will allow you to purchase for cash and to shop for the best buys, irrespective of the store you are dealing with.

Many families fail to save because they think the amount they can put aside is too insignificant. No amount is insignificant. Even $5 a month will help. Those who can should establish a surplus account in an amount that will allow them to replace things like washing machines, dryers, refrigerators, and other

Saving or Hoarding?

Be aware of the difference between savings and hoarding plans. A savings plan has a specific purpose for the money being stored; a hoarding plan is money put aside for no particular reason—money that wouldn't be spent even if it were needed.

During a time of recession in our country many of the debt-ridden people I counseled actually had a surplus of money in their savings accounts. Many of them were laid off and yet, instead of using their reserves, they used credit. Why were they saving? "Just in case." Theirs was not a savings plan, it was a hoarding plan.

Years ago, if it cost $300 to take a vacation, I would save $600. But by the time vacation time came around, I had grown so attached to the $600 that I didn't want to spend it, and so I wouldn't take a vacation. That was not a savings plan, it was a hoarding plan.

One man's goal was to save ten years' salary so that if he wanted to take ten years off, he could. His character, however, was such that if he took five days off, he got bored and would immediately go back to work. His plan was motivated primarily by fear of the future. He was doing something that had no rationale; it qualified as a hoarding plan.

appliances that will wear out. This will normally require an allocation of at least 5 percent.

STARTING A NEW BUDGET

After determining your present spending level (where you are) and reviewing the guideline percentages (where you should be), your task becomes one of developing a new budget that handles the areas of overspending.

The Budget Analysis page (figure 2.3) provides space for summarizing both actual expenses and guideline expenses. The total amounts of each category from the Monthly Income and Expense sheet (figure 2.1) and from the Budget Percentage Guidelines (figure 2.2) should be transferred to the appropriate columns on the Budget Analysis page.

Compare the "Existing Budget" and "Guideline" columns. Note the difference, plus or minus, in the "Difference" column. A negative notation indicates a deficit; a positive notation indicates a surplus.

After comparing the "Existing Budget" and "Guideline" columns, you must make some decisions about overspending. It may be possible to reduce some areas to compensate for overspending in others. For example, if housing expenditures are more than 30 percent, it may be necessary to sacrifice in such areas as entertainment and recreation, miscellaneous, and automobiles. If debts exceed 6 percent, then the problems are compounded. Ultimately, the decision becomes one of where and how to cut back.

BUDGET ANALYSIS

PER YEAR _____   NET SPENDABLE INCOME PER MONTH _____

PER MONTH _____

MONTHLY PAYMENT CATEGORY	EXISTING BUDGET	MONTHLY GUIDELINE BUDGET	DIFFERENCE + OR −	NEW MONTHLY BUDGET
1. Tithe				
2. Taxes				
NET SPENDABLE INCOME (PER MONTH)	$ _____	$ _____	$ _____	$ _____
3. Housing				
4. Food				

5. Automobile(s)				
6. Insurance				
7. Debts				
8. Enter. & Recreation				
9. Clothing				
10. Savings				
11. Medical				
12. Miscellaneous				
TOTALS (Items 3 through 12)	$ _____	$ _____		$ _____

Figure 2.3

It is not necessary that your new budget fit the guideline budget. It is necessary that your new budget not exceed Net Spendable Income. The *minimum* objective of any budget should be to meet the family's needs without creating any further debt.

It is usually at this point that husband-wife communication is so important. No one person can make a budget work because it may involve a family financial sacrifice. Without a willingness to sacrifice and establish discipline, no budget will succeed.

SUMMARY

Now you have the necessary ingredients for establishing a financial plan for your home. There is only one ingredient necessary to complete the plan—action. No plan is ever going to implement itself. It requires effort on your part— and good communication within your family.

The following is a list of the financial principles applicable to your family budget.

1. Use a written plan.
2. Provide for God's work from the first part of your income.
3. Limit your credit. Trim back as far as possible.
4. When you are considering buying new items, consider these questions before buying:
   - Is it necessary?
   - Is it the best buy you can find?
   - Is it an impulse item?

5. Practice saving money regularly. Even a small amount is a good discipline to establish.
6. Set your own goals with your family. Do not try to fit into someone else's goals.
7. Get out of debt. Make the commitment that you are going to get all your obligations to a current status.
8. Avoid indulgences and lavishness in your family life.
9. Seek good counsel if you have a question.
10. Stick to your plans diligently.
11. Avoid the use of outside tellers to get cash.
12. Avoid the use of automatic overdraft protection.
13. Balance your checkbook—to the penny *every* month.
14. Use a carbon copy checkbook if possible.
15. Have only one bookkeeper in the family.

Eight Steps to Budgets That Work

DON'T FORGET HIDDEN DEBTS!

Hidden debts usually include bills that do not come due on a monthly basis. Your budget must provide for these. If it doesn't, they will take all the surplus money for a whole month when they come due.

An example of a hidden debt is insurance that is paid on a yearly basis. The needed amount should be divided by 12 and put aside every month. Follow the same practice for clothing, automobile repairs, vacations, and medical bills. Failure to do this will ultimately wreck your budget. Other debts that are commonly overlooked are magazine subscriptions, credit owed to family or friends, fluctuating utility bills, taxes, and investments.

In addition, appliances and household goods (furniture, rugs, drapes, etc.) wear out or deteriorate over time. Periodic allocations should be made to replace those items as necessary.

Ideally, automobile depreciation and maintenance should also be allocated on a monthly basis. That savings would then pay for maintenance, insurance, and replacement of the automobile (assuming the car is kept for seven years or 140,000 miles).

The tendency in tight budgeting situations is to avoid maintenance and depreciation savings with the excuse that "we just can't afford it." Even if the full amount cannot be set aside, try to save something for those purposes. Depreciation is the same as any other expense. Without money to repair a car, the usual alternative is to replace it—on the time payment plan!

Failure to plan for short-range variables and depreciating items results in crisis planning. Control your expenditures; don't let them control you. How?

Use the table illustrated in figure 3.1 to determine how much must be allocated to the various categories. For example, if automobile insurance is $240 per year, set aside $20 per month so that the bill can be paid when due.

At the end of each month transfer the allocated money not actually used to a savings account. The savings ledger shows the various categories for which money is being saved (figure 3.2). Each account should have a predetermined limit. Once that limit has been reached, no additional savings are necessary.

Example: Assume $360 is the yearly total for medical expenses. Once the savings for medical reaches $360, the needed reserve has been met. Unless greater medical expenses are expected, savings beyond $360 is not necessary. Monthly funds can then be applied elsewhere until a medical expense occurs that reduces the amount in savings.

SAVINGS ACCOUNT ALLOCATIONS

Date	Deposit	With-draw	Bal-ance	Hous-ing	Food	Auto Insur.	Insur-ance	Clothes	Medical					

Figure 3.1

Remember, the plan is to establish a reserve for variables, depreciating items, maintenance, or special needs such as fluctuating income. The savings account ledger divides the surplus by budget category.

VARIABLE EXPENSE PLANNING

Estimated Cost per Month

1. Vacation	$ _____	÷ 12 =	$ _____
2. Dentist	$ _____	÷ 12 =	$ _____
3. Doctor	$ _____	÷ 12 =	$ _____
4. Automobile	$ _____	÷ 12 =	$ _____
5. Annual Insurance	$ _____	÷ 12 =	$ _____
(Life)	$ _____	÷ 12 =	$ _____
(Health)	$ _____	÷ 12 =	$ _____
(Auto)	$ _____	÷ 12 =	$ _____
(Home)	$ _____	÷ 12 =	$ _____
6. Clothing	$ _____	÷ 12 =	$ _____
7. Investments	$ _____	÷ 12 =	$ _____
8. Other	$ _____	÷ 12 =	$ _____

Figure 3.2

CONTROL IMPULSE SPENDING

Impulse items are the things you always want but never need. Credit cards are the primary means of buying on impulse. Therefore, if you stop the credit, you probably stop the impulse.

Impulse purchases can be very small or very large. They range from buying homes and cars

IMPULSE LIST

DATE	IMPULSE ITEM	1	2	3

Figure 3.3

to buying lunch. The price of the object is not the important issue, its necessity is. You must consider every purchase in light of your budget.

Here are some hints on how to reduce your impulse buying:

- Use a delayed purchase plan. Buy nothing outside of your budget unless you wait thirty days.
- Check and record at least two other prices within those thirty days.
- Allow only one new purchase at a time on your impulse buying record.
- Never use credit cards for impulse purchasing.

I never bought large things on impulse, but the small things were still impulse purchases. Tools were my weakness. I would go into a department store and see all kinds of tools that I never needed but always wanted. Since my budget couldn't stand the strain, I decided to break the habit.

I began by posting an impulse buying chart on my bedroom door (see Figure 3.3). I determined not to buy anything that cost $10 or more unless I waited thirty days and got two more prices. Also, I would not have more than one item on my list at a time. I continued that plan for over six months without purchasing a single item on my chart. The reason was obvious: Once I left the store, the impulse passed, and before the thirty days was out, I'd identified something else I wanted more. Later I discovered a plan that was infallible: Stay out of stores.

PLAN GIFT-GIVING

Gifts should be a part of the budget. Consider the amount you will spend on gifts every year and plan for their purchase.

Regardless of your financial status, in debt or otherwise, determine to bring gift-giving under control. Here are a few hints that may help you:

1. Keep an event calendar for the year and budget ahead. Buy on sale. Shop for birthdays and anniversaries ahead of time, so you don't have to buy quickly. Many times the cost is increased because the gift is selected at the last moment.

2. Initiate crafts within the family and make some of the needed gifts. Some examples are: wall plaques, purses, string art, macrame, and so forth. Not only will making gifts help bring your family together, but they also reflect love.

3. Draw names for selected gifts rather than giving each family member something.

4. Determine not to buy any gifts on credit (especially Christmas gifts). Credit reflects very little love. It would be much better to make something with your own hands rather than borrow in order to give.

5. Help your children earn money for gifts. You can also help your children be aware of others' needs. Perhaps they could give a gift to someone who really needs it rather than to a family member.

One Christmas a friend shared something that happened in his family. "The most valuable Christmas gift I ever received was a postcard from my children that read, 'Mom and Dad,' we love you and we've used the money for your gift to feed the poor this year. Your loving children.' "

6. Consider sending cards on special birthdays and anniversaries rather than presents. Cards reflect as much love as any other gift and sometimes more.

WATCH MISCELLANEOUS SPENDING

Most counselors have heard this response from couples who have filled out budget forms: "I know we don't spend that much money. Where does it all go every month?" A great deal of it probably goes into "Miscellaneous."

One of the purposes of a budget is to control miscellaneous spending and evaluate where the fixed spending is excessive. There will never be "enough" money in the budget until spending is under control.

A few years ago I met a surgeon who confirmed this principle for me. He earned $180,000 a year and had done so for approximately ten years, yet he was always in debt. The doctor's early years were interesting. He had grown up in an orphanage, worked through four years of college in virtual poverty, worked four years in med school in virtual poverty, spent four years in residency training in virtual poverty, and then suddenly had an income of more than $100,000 a year.

He didn't think that anyone could spend that much money. However, anyone can spend *any* amount of money. It may take more ingenuity after $100,000, but it can certainly be done, and he proved it.

After a conference in his city, I received a telephone call from him. "The next time you are in my city, I would really like to have a chance to talk to you. I think I have a problem," he said. I asked him if he would mind describing a little bit about the problem. "Last month I made $27,000 and spent $32,000." I agreed that he really did have a problem.

A few weeks later, I was in his area again and called to set up a meeting. I wanted to discern exactly what the problem was and what could be done about it. As I went through his records, I found he had his office, his home, and everything else requiring money all linked together. His receptionist, who was also his bookkeeper, paid all the bills. For the month in question, I found that he had spent $7,600 on a jeep for his son, who had wrecked it without insurance coverage, and the doctor had bought him another one. His wife had decided she wanted to grow some flowers that month, so she had a greenhouse built for $14,000. It went on and on. When I asked him about these expenditures, he said, "But that was an abnormal month. That couldn't happen every month."

As we looked back over the previous five or six months, it seemed that something equivalent had happened every month. He had so much money in oil wells that he could have bought part of Texas.

He had almost convinced me that he could

control his spending without drastic measures until we walked into his backyard and I saw an airplane without wings. I asked him, "Why in the world do you have an airplane in your backyard? Does anyone in your family fly?" He said, "No, nobody flies, but a long time ago a fellow sold me that airplane because it would be a good depreciating asset." I congratulated him on the selection of that investment because it really had depreciated — in his backyard.

As we began developing a budget, I found that he could have lived on $30,000 a year and maintained the same standard of living. Obviously, he couldn't have bought the new cars, jeeps, greenhouses, or all the other indulgences he was involved with, including several "get-rich-quick" programs.

He and his wife settled on a budget of $40,000 a year. Before I left I said to his receptionist, "If he wants to get *any* more money, give me a call first."

During the next months, the family lived within its budget simply by adjusting spending to the necessary rather than the lavish. After eight or nine months I received a call from the good doctor, and he was literally beaming. "I've found that we have our spending under control and three things have happened as a result. Number one, I am able to reduce the fees in my practice. Number two, we are able to have surplus money and use it for both our family and the Lord's work. Best of all, though, we have peace in our lives for the first time ever."

DIVIDE RESPONSIBILITIES
IN THE HOME

It is important for both husband and wife to recognize their joint responsibilities in the home. It is sometimes assumed that the family budget is the husband's responsibility. That simply is not true. If the wife in the home can manage finances better than the husband, then she ought to be the bookkeeper. In fact, wives are the bookkeepers in over 90 percent of the homes.

This does not mean that when finances are in a mess the husband asks his wife to bail them out. They must both sit down, divide the responsibilities for the home finances, and decide who can best handle what.

Deciding how money should be divided into various categories such as clothing, groceries, automobiles, insurance, and so forth, is also a job for both husband and wife. They should create a compatible, cooperative plan, not one based on one individual's whims.

Husband and wife may not always agree on everything in the budget. If two people always agree on everything one of them is unnecessary. The principle to observe is reasonable compromise. What's fair for one must be fair for the other.

After I have helped a family establish a budget, I will ask them to come back in a month or two. When they come, I ask the question, "How do you like your budget?" The response is often the same. The husband says, "Oh, I love it. It gives us more surplus money than we've ever had before." So I ask the wife, "How do you like it?" To which she replies, "It's terrible, it's so confining I can hardly stand it. I never have any free money."

I know what has happened. The husband has established a budget for his wife so confining that nobody could live with it, but he has an expense account or some other source of money to fall back on. Whenever the pressure is too great, he'll go out and eat breakfast or lunch on his expense account. Meanwhile, his wife is suffering without such a luxury. That kind of a budget will not last. It's phony.

Your budget should be a plan to bring peace, not conflict, into your home. If you as husband and wife find that you cannot create a budget and agree on it by yourselves, consult a pastor or a counselor in Christian financial service. Ask him to help you develop a budget and use him as a sounding board. Christian Financial Concepts has trained several hundred volunteer counselors in churches throughout America. We will be glad to provide a list of those in your area if you are unable to locate one on your own.

DEVELOP GOOD RECORDS
It is impossible to manage your money without keeping good financial records. These include:

- A good double entry ledger where all checks and bank expenses are posted.
- A ledger type checkbook where *all* checks are posted when written. A carbon copy

checkbook is an excellent safeguard against unrecorded checks.
- A budget book defining the amounts to be spent on each household expense each month.

In addition, it is impossible to have a home budget without balancing your checkbook. If you cannot balance your records, ask your bank account manager for his help. Here are some things that you should do to help keep a good checkbook:

1. Use a ledger type checkbook (as opposed to a stub type).
2. Before you tear out the first check, write in every check number.
3. Before you tear out a check, record the information in the ledger.
4. Either husband or wife should keep the ledger and the checkbook so that only one person is actually making entries.
5. Balance the ledger every month without exception. If you don't know how to balance your checking account, the procedure is usually shown on the backside of your monthly bank statement.

GET OUT OF DEBT

How do you begin the process of getting out of debt? Once you know exactly how much you owe, the next step is to list all your obligations, from the largest to the smallest. The total obligations will equal 100 percent of your debt. Determine what percentage each of your cred-

LIST OF DEBTS

TO WHOM OWED	CONTACT PHONE NO.	PAY OFF	PAYMENTS REMAINING	MONTHLY PAYMENT	DATE

Figure 3.4

itors represents. For instance, the largest may be 25 percent, and the second may be 20 percent, the third 15 percent, the fourth 10 percent, and so on. This determination lets you know how to allocate the funds to each creditor, which brings you to the next step.

Contact your creditors. You should make personal contact with every single creditor on your list. Send them not only a copy of your budget but also a copy of your breakdown so that they will know exactly how much money you can allocate to them on a monthly basis. Even though you might have been committed to paying more than you have available, you can pay only what is available. The chart on page 62 will assist you in making these contacts and keeping records.

Reduce your debts. I recommend that you list each of your debts on a three-by-five-inch card. Take the smallest debt, whether it be $5 or $50, and post that three-by-five-inch card on your bathroom mirror, so that every time you look at it you will be reminded to pray about that specific debt and do something specific and constructive about it.

Place a small can in your bedroom for the change allocated to paying off that debt, and every time you have some change in your pocket, put it in the can, and begin to reduce that debt.

Use at least 50 percent of any "windfall" income to pay existing debts. Windfall income can be gifts, overtime, garage sales, part-time work, etc.

One of your greatest rewards is seeing those debts begin to dissolve. As they do, write across your cards "An Answer to Prayer." As you pay off the one debt, put the money you were paying on it into the second debt. When you have paid off the second debt, do the same for the third debt, and so on. In time you will be totally out of debt.

Stick to your priorities. You may have to sacrifice to get current. You may need to reduce credit buying and seek alternate ways of satisfying needs. You may need to repair the refrigerator or washing machine you were going to trade. You may need to surrender vacation money to your creditors. Whatever you must do to bring your debt burden back under control, determine your priorities and stick to them.

Beware of more borrowing. Consolidation loans, refinancing, and more loans are *not* solutions; they merely treat the "symptoms."

Destroy credit cards. No, you do not *need* credit cards. You may want credit cards; many people desire them. But for those who are in debt, it is an absolute necessity to do without them.

If you don't have a paper slicer around your house, and you decide to get rid of your cards, just preheat your oven to 400 degrees and throw them in. (No, not really. It will smell up your home.)

SET FAMILY GOALS

Goal No. 1: Trust. A couple came for counseling and one of the questions worrying the wife was, "Our income is substantially reduced from what it was for the last few years. How will we ever buy another home? We don't even have the down payment for one."

The only answer I had was, "What a great opportunity to put your trust in God into practice. God knows your needs and specializes in the impossible. You must have enough faith to believe that if God wishes you to have a home, He will supply it."

This young couple had moved into a condominium they simply couldn't afford. The move from at $240-a-month apartment to a $600-a-month condominium had wiped out their savings and income as well. They were forced to give up the condominium and move back into an apartment. The attitude of the wife was, "I don't think I can live in another apartment. I know we may never get another home."

We prayed about their problem, turned it over to God, and they began to search for God's direction. Before two months had gone by, they received a call from a friend who was going to India for two years as a medical missionary. He had a large home with almost every available luxury and asked if they would mind living in the house to maintain it during his absence. If they consented, he would provide them with free rent. God provided a home they could never have afforded at a price they could.

Goal No. 2: Savings. The amount of money set aside in a savings will vary from family to family. On an average, it will probably be between $1,500 and $3,000. This savings account can be used to purchase necessary appliances, pay for car repairs, and so forth.

The purpose of a savings account is not for

"protection." It is to help you be a better steward of God's resources by removing the necessity for credit cards.

Goal No. 3: Family Sharing Time. An essential part of every Christian family's growth is a family sharing time. This should be a regularly scheduled time when both husband and wife go over the financial matters of the week, including the needs of the children, the chores that were or were not accomplished, and the rewards or punishments that are going to be handed out.

Keep a chart on the specific tasks you assign your children so that each can measure his or her progress. It is also a good check of your own faithfulness in rewarding or punishing justly. You should establish the discipline that all family members will be present at the same time.

Consistency on the part of the parents is all important. If you establish 8:00 P.M. as the time to study God's Word and discuss problems, your children should recognize that their responsibility is to be there, on time! One of the ways you will know when your family time is meeting the needs of your family is when your children remind *you*.

Goal No. 4: Husband-Wife Time. As necessary as time with the children is, even more essential is time spent with your spouse. The two of you should spend time together on a regular basis, and not only after 11:00 P.M. It may mean sacrificing some outside activities, but it is vital that you begin to communicate and get to know each other. The only way to do so is by dedicating time to each other.

You should have some guidelines for your time together, including specific short-range goals you're trying to accomplish.

Goal No. 5: Ministry to Other People. As your finances improve, begin a ministry to others around you. These can be your neighbors, Christian associates, or co-workers.

Show other couples the plans you have applied to your life and the effect they have had. Try to allow at least one night a month to help another couple who is having similar problems.

As you are available to others, you will find that God will bring those with needs.

The Power of Prayer

Several years ago I met Warren, who had just lost his real estate business. At the time he owed over $200,000 and didn't have a job.

As we talked I realized very quickly there was nothing I could do to help him. So we stopped and simply prayed, "God, please rescue him."

Warren made out a budget based on the needs of his family and the needs of his creditors. Next, he contacted all his creditors, sending each one a copy of his budget. He told them that he simply did not have any money to pay them, but if they would wait, he would pay them all he could, when he could.

A miracle happened. That year, just before Christmas, one of the banks to whom he owed nearly $100,000 decided to write off his debt as a tax loss and told him not to pay it.

About nine months later, he had a second call from the same bank. One of the investments he had pledged as collateral had been sold. Not only was there enough money to pay off the indebtedness of approximately $80,000, but there was enough to yield nearly $40,000 extra.

In a little less than one year, Warren had gone from over $200,000 in debt to debt free. He continues to live on the same budget that he established during that first year. He found, as most of us do, that the high cost of living was not his problem, but the cost of living high.

Long-Range Plans: Insurance and Retirement

LIFE INSURANCE

Life insurance falls into two basic categories: cash value and term.

Cash value insurance. This type of insurance is known also as whole life, universal life, permanent insurance, or any number of other trade names. Its basic feature is that it is usually purchased for an individual's lifetime and accumulates some cash reserve from the paid-in premium.

Cash value insurance is relatively expensive initially. In any family with limited funds available it is usually so costly that the family ends up underinsured. If the wage earner dies unexpectedly, the family can quickly exhaust the available resources. I usually recommend term insurance for younger families with limited funds.

Term insurance. Term insurance means insurance that is sold for a determinable number of years. Most term policies do not accumulate any cash reserves and therefore the premium costs increase at each renewal

How Much Life Insurance?

This is a difficult question to answer precisely. There are many variables within each family that must be considered, such as: the age of the children, the spouse's income capability, existing debts, current life-style and income, and any other sources of after-death income besides life insurance. One family may wish to supply enough insurance to live off interest income alone while another may wish to provide for a specific number of years. These decisions should be made mutually by husband and wife.

One method to help you evaluate how much insurance you need is based on present income and spending. Once you have begun to budget, the same income would probably be necessary in the event of the wage earner's death.

Using the following guide, we will assume that a man dies, leaving a wife and two young children. His annual income had been $25,000. He had no large investment plan and only a small savings plan.

Husband's annual income $25,000
Less:
Insurance cost (not necessary) $500
Savings (not necessary) $1,000
His living costs $3,000
Social Security income $10,000
Wife's part-time income $2,500

After-death income available (or expenses no longer needed) ($17,000)

Income needed for family $8,000

Multiply $8,000 × 12.5 = $100,000.00 insurance needed. (Multiplying the amount needed yearly by 12.5 yields the approximate amount of insurance necessary to earn $8,000 yearly at 8% interest. Thus, the approximate amount of insurance necessary to earn $8,000 in interest income is $100,000.)

If additional funds are needed for education or other special circumstances, these should also be considered. Remember that *balance* must be the key here. Don't overprotect your family. The true purpose of life insurance is to *provide* for a family after the death of the income producer, not "protect" it against the future or serve as a savings or retirement plan.

period. There are two basic types of term insurance: decreasing term and level term. In decreasing term the cost (payment) stays constant but the face value or payment decreases annually. In level term the cost increases for the period selected while the face value stays the same. Simply stated:

Decreasing term = consistent cost and decreasing payout.

Level term = increasing cost and constant payout.

Which type of term is best for family needs? I believe level term is better because the need for insurance in a family does not decrease at a predictable rate as the decreasing term policy does.

For example, assume that a twenty-five-year-old father of two young children bought a $25,000 decreasing term policy. In ten years his policy would be worth approximately $20,000 but his insurance needs would not have declined; in fact, they may well have increased.

With a level term policy his premiums would have increased but the insurance coverage remained the same. Additional coverage could be purchased when needed.

A cost comparison. Is cash value insurance actually less expensive than term insurance over the long run?

It is noteworthy that most cash value policies at some point actually accumulate more cash reserves per year than the yearly premiums while term insurance rates continue to increase. Unless the early years' savings are invested and used to pay the premiums later, the cost of the term can become prohibitively high.

Probably the best way to summarize life insurance by cost and type is to look at how much money is available to purchase what you need.

Most young families can afford *only* term life insurance. Term is much less expensive initially than cash value insurance. The older the insured person is, the more costly the term policy. If a significant amount of savings is not

Choose Your Agent Wisely

One of your best assets is a good, independent insurance agent to help you with your decisions. Shop around—a lot! Look for an agent who has your interests at heart and not his own. If you share many of the ideas that I have shared with you, some insurance agents will insist, "It isn't true." But the proof should be in black and white. Ask them to thoroughly define their insurance plan in writing and then have several other agents give you a comparative price.

established by thirty to forty years of age, it's best to look to cash value insurance for the later years.

HEALTH INSURANCE

The matter of health insurance is too complex to do more than touch on here. There is virtually no way to evaluate health insurance policies because each is usually tailored to individual clients or companies.

The cost of health insurance is generally excessive except for employees covered by a group (company) medical plan. For those who are not covered in this way, a major medical plan is probably best. Major medical insurance is basically catastrophe coverage. It will exclude perhaps the initial $250 to $500 of medical expenses and then pay 80 or 90 percent of medical expenses above the deductible. The actual cost of a major medical policy is often much less than individual health insurance that pays after the initial $100.

With this type of insurance it is necessary that you have access to enough money to pay the deductible. Thus your long-range planning should provide savings for this purpose.

Shopping for cost and value is very important with health insurance. You will find that virtually identical policies may vary as much as 25 percent from one major insurance company to the next.

DISABILITY INSURANCE

As with health insurance, it is almost impossible to describe the different types of disability insurance. An agent can virtually design a policy on the spot if you can afford it.

Balance is again most important. You must ask yourself whether your attitude is motivated by fear of the unknown or by God's plan for your family. A pressure salesman can generate an attitude of fear by describing "horror stories" that happened to other families. But you must develop your own plans, which may or may not include disability insurance. In no case should disability insurance be looked upon as a means to supply all future income. The cost would be so high that it would rob current family needs, and even worse, take away the incentive to readjust to a new life.

Phil recently came to me asking for help in getting his home budget into shape. "I just can't seem to make ends meet," was the answer he gave to my question about his problem.

Phil was an airline pilot and made a substantial salary. It was quite sufficient to have a sizeable surplus available if handled properly. There were several areas of his budget that needed a bit more control, but the area of insurance was completely out of proportion.

He had enough life insurance to provide for two or three families in the event of his death and enough disability insurance to triple his income if he lost his pilot's license. I asked him what terrible thing would cause him to lose his pilot's license. "Would you have to suffer a heart attack or have a leg cut off?"

"No, it could be eyesight, or blood pressure, or even a loss of hearing," he said. "But if I did lose my license I wouldn't know how to do anything."

My question to Phil was, "Would you be willing to lie in bed the rest of your life with your eyes closed? If not, why plan your life as if you intend to?"

He reduced his life insurance to a reasonable amount and trimmed his disability insurance to the amount necessary for provision rather than profit. In doing so he freed almost $300 a month.

RETIREMENT
In our society it seems that more people are worried about retiring than working. Young

workers in the job market establish as their major criteria for employment security and good retirement benefits.

Many people today work through their most productive years at a job they can hardly stand only because it has a good retirement plan. Later most of them find that retirement isn't all it's cracked up to be. There are no retirement plans that can replace thirty or forty wasted years.

I knew an individual with a government agency whose job requirement had been eliminated for ten years. With no job responsibilities, his single function each day was to cross off another block on his planning calendar. "One more day closer to retirement," he would say.

What a waste of life. His entire life spent in the future. Although his case is extreme, it is not unusual. Many others are falling into the trap of this same nonsense.

Before most of us who were born after 1930 are of retirement age the whole system may be drastically revised. Rather than total retirement, it will probably be necessary to adopt a modified retirement plan that will provide continuing income.

As you are considering your retirement goals you should not rob the family of current needs in prospect of some elusive "rainy day." Perhaps the following explanations of some of the more common individual retirement plans will help you decide on realistic goals.

Annuities. An annuity, created specifically for retirement, is an investment plan into which the purchaser pays a scheduled amount of money each year with the agreement that he or she will receive a lifetime income upon retirement. A portion of the payout is tax-free at retirement.

The amount of payout is determined by the sum of money paid in. For instance, a person age thirty who paid $50 a month until age sixty-five would naturally receive a larger annuity than a person who began paying in the same amount at age forty-five.

There are innumerable modifications available on annuities, but basically they relate to two classes of annuity: fixed and variable payout. The fixed annuity guarantees a specific amount per month from retirement age until death. The variable annuity can adjust the payout depending on the earnings of the fund from year to year.

A fixed annuity is generally better for those approaching retirement—say within fifteen years—while the variable annuity is better suited for younger participants. The reason is that with the steady increase in inflation, a fixed annuity for a younger family may be inadequate by the time it matures. Thus the variable feature provides the capability to adjust with inflation.

There are also charitable annuities created by charitable organizations where a portion of the monthly installment is tax deductible and upon the death of the beneficiary the principle goes to the charity—a good use of money.

Endowment policies. This plan is similar to an annuity in that the purchaser agrees to pay a given amount per year until retirement age and in return is guaranteed a fixed monthly payout for life. Be sure to check the "guaranteed" rate on the policy against the projected rate. Quite often the guaranteed rate is far less than that offered by high-quality bonds or other securities.

Mutual funds. The basic purpose of a mutual fund is to combine the investment dollars of many people and buy securities in large dollar amounts.

Because of the sums of money involved, it is possible to employ expert counsel to handle the investments. Some companies charge an initial fee to handle the investment (called front loaders), while others charge a percentage of earnings. It is preferable to use a company that takes its fee from earnings. That way it assumes some risk just as the investor does.

A mutual fund is a long-range investment plan and has the capability to adjust earnings through investments in stocks and bonds. Therefore, losses are also possible.

Most mutual funds can be shifted from investments primarily in stocks to investments primarily in bonds. Since bonds or money funds have guaranteed payouts, the mutual fund can therefore be converted into a relatively conservative investment.

The best advice possible is to *shop*. Check with several agents of mutual fund companies and compare their plans. You should insist that their proposals be made in writing (and in English) so that you can compare them.

There are many other types of retirement plans available, including government retirement, social security, and corporate security. To better understand these you should ask your independent insurance agent for the appropriate brochures. If you cannot fully understand them, seek counsel from someone working in that area.

Cost-Saving Tips

FOOD

- Don't take your children grocery shopping. A child in a grocery store is like an octopus. A two year old sitting in a shopping basket seems to be able to reach candies and cookies four feet away. The pressures of your children will almost always force you to buy things you otherwise would not.
- Never go to the grocery store hungry. Hungry shoppers buy foods that satisfy whims rather than budgets.
- Shop food sales, particularly canned goods and bulk lot specials. Begin to establish a surplus of money from which you can draw to buy in quantity.
- Always use a written list of needs.
- Avoid buying non-grocery items in a grocery supermarket except on sale. These are normally "high markup" items.
- Avoid processed and sugar-coated cereals. These are expensive and have little nutritional value. Also avoid prepared foods, such as TV dinners, pot pies, cakes, etc. You are

paying for expensive labor that you can provide.

- Determine good meat cuts that are available from roasts or shoulders and have the butcher cut these for you. Buying steaks by the package on sale is fairly inexpensive also.
- Try house brand canned products. These are normally cheaper and just as nutritious.
- Avoid products in a cyclical price hike. Substitute or eliminate them from your shopping list.
- Shop for advertised specials. These are usually posted in the store window.
- Avoid stores that give merchandise stamps if their prices reflect the cost of the stamps. (Not all do – some simply substitute stamps for other advertising.)
- Purchase milk, bread, eggs, etc., from specialty outlet stores if available, as prices are usually 10 to 15 percent lower. Keep some dry milk on hand to reduce "quick" trips to the store.

HOUSING

- When house shopping, look for an older house that can be improved by your own labor. Older houses can sometimes be purchased for much less than new ones, and family labor will enhance its worth.
- Look into areas that are not currently building. Areas that are building usually have plenty of traffic from people looking for homes and therefore command higher prices.

- Check into areas that others consider to be less desirable. Don't be swayed by what others tell you. Make your own decisions.
- Look for a small basic home that doesn't have all the frills the more expensive models do. The price of a house is increased generally because of the conveniences put into it. Many builders offer buyers the option of doing some of the finishing work themselves. This will often save several hundred dollars on the price of the home.
- Select a home that suits the *current needs* of your family. Don't try to plan for a lifetime in the first home you buy.

AUTOMOBILES
- Whenever possible *save* the money first. If you obviously cannot buy for cash and must use credit, negotiate for the car on a cash basis with no trade-in.
- When you have settled on the price for the car, go to your bank, borrow the money, and buy the car for cash. Then sell your old car yourself. You'll save a significant amount of money as opposed to trading in your old car and financing through the dealer. If you still owe on your old car, don't trade.
- Explore ways to borrow, including loans against your savings accounts, stocks or bonds, or other assets. Such loans can often save nearly half of the interest charged for auto financing.
- Decide if you really need a new car. Some people, such as those in sales, need new cars

frequently; most of us do not.
- If you're a Christian, pray before you buy a car, and let God direct you to the right one.

ENTERTAINMENT AND RECREATION
- Rather than taking a long traveling vacation, find some place closer where you can relax. Or contact another family in the area where you are going and try to arrange a swap of residences for the vacation time.
- If part of your family's recreation is eating out, you might consider instead inviting friends over for meals.
- Plan vacations during "off" seasons if possible.
- Consider a camping vacation to avoid motel and food expenses. You might pool the expenses of camping items with friends.
- Use family games in place of movies.
- If you are flying, use the least expensive coach fare (i.e., late night or early morning usually saves 10 to 20 percent).

CLOTHING
- If you have children who are thirteen or older, allow them to buy some of their own clothing. Give them a budget and let them select their own clothes. You'll find your children treat clothes differently when they are responsible for them.
- Make as many of the children's clothes as time will allow. Average savings is 50 to 60 percent.

- Make a written list of clothing needs and purchase during the "off" season as much as possible.
- Select outfits that can be mixed and used in multiple combinations rather than as a single set.
- Frequent the discount outlets that carry unmarked "name brand" goods.
- Frequent authentic factory outlet stores for closeouts of top quality items.
- Select home washable fabrics in new clothes.
- Use coin-operated dry cleaning machines instead of commercial cleaners.
- Practice early repair for damaged clothing.

MEDICAL AND DENTAL EXPENSES

- Get an annual checkup. Perhaps the best money you'll ever spend is on an annual physical. As your physician develops a yearly profile on your health, he will be able to spot changes that are signals for major health problems.
- Practice preventive medicine. Give your body the right amount of sleep, exercise, and nutrition, and it will respond with good health. Your teeth will also respond to care.
- Teach your children proper dental care, including the use of dental floss.
- Do not be hesitant to question doctors and dentists in advance about costs. Also, educate yourself enough to discern when you are getting good value for your money. Most ethical professional men will not take offense

at your questions. If they do, that may be a hint to change services.

- In the case of prescriptions, shop around. You will be amazed to discover the wide variance in prices from one store to the next. Ask about cash discounts, too. Many stores will give 5 to 10 percent off for cash purchases.
- Ask God to remove the worry and anxiety caused by finances. You'll find that both your financial life and physical life will improve.

A Savvy Shopper's Guide to Advertising

A smart shopper avoids excessive expenditures by being aware of the four main techniques used by advertisers.

1. *Would you deprive your family?* This little gimmick contrasts two buyers: Fearful Freddie, who never takes a chance and therefore never provides family wife with a microwave oven or a garbage compactor; and Successful Sam, who steps out on credit and is able to provide the "better life" for his family.

2. *Sex appeal.* This approach is used to promote specific product lines such as clothes, jewelry, perfumes, and even cars. Often it is employed by large chain stores to advertise their products. Since nobody wants to be left out or out of style, the need for these things is created. For those who cannot afford new clothes in the latest styles, the store conveniently provides credit cards.

Sales people become so accustomed to credit card buyers that when someone pays by cash, subtle pressure is applied to encourage the cash buyer to apply for a store credit card.

Statistics tell us that credit card shoppers buy an average of 25 percent more goods at an average sales price 10 to 15 percent higher than do cash shoppers.

3. *Super Sale—prices rolled back.* Here is the ultimate shopper's trap: a sale item. Most stores run continual sales. Some sale items are excellent buys and can help significantly in reducing costs. Many sale items, however, are "loss-leaders," items sold at little or no profit to draw buyers into the store, particularly credit card shoppers. Since many of these sale items are inexpensive high volume goods, the merchant knows that additional purchases will be made. After all, most credit card shoppers won't charge just four or five dollars. Other nonsale goods will be combined with the sale items to increase the total.

4. *Strategic layout.* Few people are aware of the science of store merchandising. The placement of items on the shelves is not by chance, nor is their location. Many surveys are run on the products women buy and the usual routes they take through the stores. Chain food stores, for instance, arrange most of the "junk" (into this group I lump candies, colas, and other assorted tasty habits) on the most convenient shelves. Many people wouldn't put those items into a full basket but would put them into an empty one.

Have you ever noticed that all of the convenience foods are located between knee and shoulder height? This location is intentional—consumers don't have to strain to reach the items.

All this is not done only for credit buyers. Obviously, the system was in use long before credit cards. But it is a fact that the consumption of "junk food" has increased dramatically with the use of credit. A strategic layout system is utilized in nearly every industry that sells to consumers.

I shared this observation with a couple and was not surprised to hear the wife refute the whole idea. Obviously the strategy would be useless if the buyers recognized the plan, wouldn't it?

So I encouraged her husband to go grocery shopping with her one week. The events leading up to this decision had evolved from budget talks I had held involving buying groceries. The wife had settled on one figure for groceries and her husband on another. They compromised in the middle, and he decided to help her live within their budget.

As they entered the store, the wife selected a shopping cart and, true to habit, began to advance down the nearest aisle selecting various food items. Her husband's job was to add up the purchases on a pocket calculator. They had progressed down five of the eight aisles when he announced that they had reached their budgeted amount. Amid rigorous protests, he pushed his wife toward the checkout line and departed with the next two weeks' supply of food.

Unfortunately, the food disappeared faster than time did, and they ran out of eatables the following week. Determined to stick it out for two weeks, they consumed their stock of canned goods to stretch the meals.

Finally, it was grocery day again. This time they assaulted the store with grocery list in hand. Instead of traveling the usual route, they went down the middle aisles first. They bypassed products that were lavishly decorated as well as those for which the price was not given in comparative figures (such as five cents per ounce). They eliminated all paper products (except toilet paper) as well as all sugar products and prepared foods.

This time they circled the entire store and still had money left over. The agreement was that anything saved from the food budget was the wife's personal windfall. Later, this had to be modified slightly when it was found they were having more windfall than food.

Once she knew how to shop and what to avoid, this wife became an excellent budgeter. She is now a strong advocate for consumer awareness.

For other materials available from Larry Burkett, please write Christian Financial Concepts, P.O. Box 2100, Cumming, Georgia 30130.

About the Author

LARRY BURKETT has written eight financial books, including *How to Manage Your Money* and *Your Finances in Changing Times*.

Burkett founded a nonprofit organization, Christian Financial Concepts, in 1976 to teach Christians biblical principles for managing money. Today, as president of Christian Financial Concepts, he writes, teaches seminars, and hosts a daily radio program, "How to Manage Your Money," which is heard on more than 540 stations internationally.

Burkett lives with his wife, Judy, in Dahlonega, Georgia. They have four grown children and two grandchildren.

More Help for Your Family Finances from
Larry Burkett

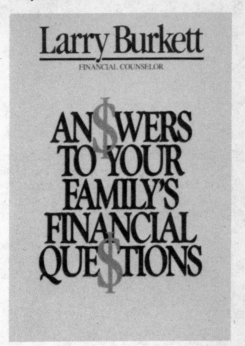

Available at your local Christian bookstore.

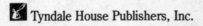

POCKET GUIDES
FROM TYNDALE

• **The Best Way to Plan Your Day** by Edward Dayton and Ted Engstrom. With the guidelines in this book, you can learn to effectively set goals, determine priorities, and beat the time crunch. 72-0373-1

• **Christianity: Hoax or History?** by Josh McDowell. Was Jesus Christ a liar, a lunatic, or Lord? A popular speaker and author looks at the resurrection of Jesus and other claims of the Christian faith. 72-0367-7

• **Demons, Witches, and the Occult** by Josh McDowell and Don Stewart. Why are people fascinated with the occult? This informative guide will answer your questions about occult practices and their dangers. 72-0541-6

• **Facing Your Fears** by Norm Wright. A guide that gives specific help for those struggling with the fears of intimacy, failure, and losing control. 72-0825-3

• **Family Budgets That Work** by Larry Burkett. Customize a budget for your household with the help of this hands-on workbook. By the host of the radio talk show "How to Manage Your Money." 72-0829-6

• **Getting Out of Debt** by Howard L. Dayton, Jr. At last, a no-nonsense approach to your money problems. Here's advice on creating a budget, cutting corners, making investments, and paying off loans. 72-1004-5

• **How to Really Love Your Job** by Don Osgood. A guide that offers practical advice for the in-a-rut employee who wants more job satisfaction. 72-2830-0

• **Make Your Dream Come True** by Charles Swindoll. These ten inspirational chapters will lead any man or woman in the quest for inner strength and growth and help develop great character traits. 72-7007-2

POCKET GUIDES
FROM TYNDALE

• **Maximize Your Mid-Life** by Jim and Sally Conway. Readers will learn to recognize the warning signs of a crisis and discover the ingredients to a strong mid-life marriage. 72-4197-8

• **The Perfect Way to Lose Weight** by Charles Kuntzleman and Daniel Runyon. Anyone can lose fat—and keep it off permanently. This tested program, developed by a leading physical fitness expert, shows how. 72-4935-9

• **Preparing for Childbirth** by Debra Evans. Expectant moms can replace their fears about childbirth with joyful anticipation. Includes suggestions for preparing for labor, breastfeeding, and more that will benefit both mothers and fathers. 72-4917-0

• **Raising Teenagers Right** by James Dobson. Dr. Dobson, an authority on child development, answers some of the most-asked questions about the teenage years: how to implement discipline, build confidence, and discuss puberty. 72-5139-6

• **Sex, Guilt & Forgiveness** by Josh McDowell. This book offers practical counsel on learning to forgive oneself and others following sexual experiences outside of marriage. 72-5908-7

• **Six Attitudes for Winners** by Norman Vincent Peale. Let an internationally known speaker and author help you replace fear, worry, apathy, and despair with courage, peace, hope, and enthusiasm. 72-5906-0

• **Skeptics Who Demanded a Verdict** by Josh McDowell. Three convincing stories of faith from some famous skeptics: C.S. Lewis, Charles Colson, and Josh McDowell. 72-5925-7

P O C K E T   G U I D E S
F R O M   T Y N D A L E